FARMERS UNITE!

PLANTING A PROTEST FOR FAIR PRICES

LINDSAY H. METCALF

CALKINS CREEK
AN IMPRINT OF
BOYDS MILLS & KANE
New York

For Dad

—LHM

Title Page: Farmers seeking parity—a selling price above the cost of crop production—park near the US Capitol, February 5, 1979.

Farmers strike to demand fair crop prices, Plains, Georgia, 1977.

FARMERS IN 1977

had a problem: they were going broke.

Crop prices tanked. Expenses soared for tractors, fuel, and land.

"When a bushel of wheat costs me $3.20 cents to raise and the selling price is around $2.40, something is wrong," said Fred Bartels, a Colorado farmer.

To survive, farmers got creative.

Some paid for haircuts with corn. Many stored grain, awaiting better prices.

"You bet we started crying in our milk," said Marjory Scheufler of Kansas.

Whispers spread over morning coffee about father-son operations that folded. About newspapers advertising six farm auctions at a time.

If this kept up, who would be left to feed the nation?

"Apathy is going to destroy us," Scheufler said.

After the fall harvest, the farmers planted a plan . . .

Midnight farm strike,
Washington, DC, December 14, 1977

. . . to send in the tractors.

About twenty thousand farmers flooded tiny Plains, Georgia, hoping to catch President Jimmy Carter, a peanut grower, at home over Thanksgiving. Two weeks later, one hundred thousand tractors paraded to state capitals around the country in protest of unfair crop prices.

The new American Agriculture Movement (AAM) spread "faster [than] crab grass," Scheufler said.

These first "tractorcades" energized farmers for the next step—to remind lawmakers in Washington, DC, that food doesn't grow in grocery stores.

The farmers grew a bold plan . . .

Plains, Georgia, November 1977

. . . to send in the tractors.

In January 1979, a rainbow of machines roared toward the nation's capital from all types of farms—grain to poultry to cotton.

"We've got to have some relief and have it now," said Tommy Kersey, a Georgia peanut farmer.

Parades rumbled thirty miles long across flatlands, over mountains, and through clogged-up cities.

Near the Tennessee–Virginia state line

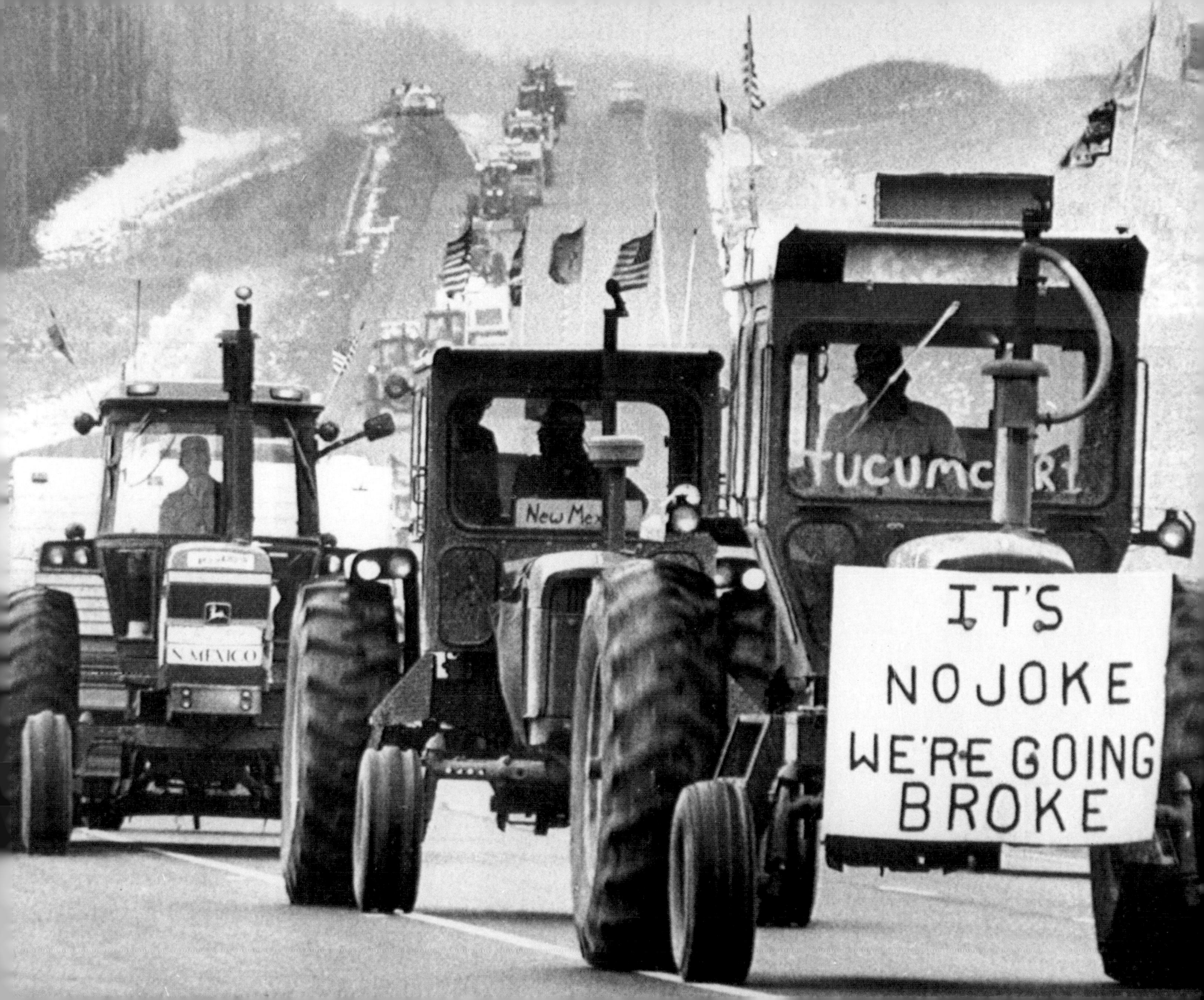
N MEXICO
New Mex
TUCUMCARI
IT'S
NO JOKE
WE'RE GOING
BROKE

"This is the worst traffic jam I've ever seen," a helicopter newsman told Kansas City radio listeners.

Flags flapped. Signs screamed. "The Battle Hymn of the Republic" blared. The tractors rolled along for weeks, until February 5, 1979, when up to ten thousand vehicles—tractors, trucks, and campers—trampled through rush hour toward Capitol Hill.

Walt Hillard, Kansas farmer

Traffic snarled. Police scowled. Towering tractors jammed commuter routes to a standstill, turning DC into Tractor Town.

"We only want to get a fair wage for our work," said George Burrows of Kansas.

"They lost my vote," a man said of the farmers after he arrived an hour late to work.

Whitehurst Freeway, Washington, DC,
February 5, 1979

David Senter, an American Agriculture Movement leader in Texas, along with Marcus Everidge, a farmer from Georgia, chained their tractors at the US Department of Agriculture. There the tractors would stay until someone "guarantees us something better than what we've got," Everidge said.

With the tractors secured, they marched to the Capitol steps for a rally.

US Department of Agriculture administration building

Thirty thousand farmers and allies gathered in DC, eager to exercise their voices in peaceful protest.

They promised parades every day. "Get 'em rollin' and keep 'em going," said Joe Flanagan of Texas.

But the city couldn't handle much more tractor traffic. While the farmers rallied, police plotted a plan . . .

American Agriculture Movement rally, US Capitol

. . . to lure in the tractors.

Police waved the farmers toward the National Mall, as if to say:

This way! Free parking! Green space here!

Then, with the tractors cornered, dozens of city dump trucks, garbage trucks, buses, police cars, and vans corralled them like cattle.

"Our boys just fenced in that stampedin' herd," a DC driver jeered.

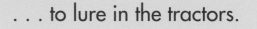

Approaching the Washington Monument

Tractors on the National Mall

"We come here trying to do something for this country and they treat us like this," said Larry Schmitz of Kansas.

Police told the protestors not to worry. They would allow small, out-of-the-way parades each day.

But would that be enough?

Police surround a tractor in Washington, DC.

Farmers like Ken Ochsner had crawled sixteen hundred miles to be seen, not to be barricaded behind buses. Back home in Kansas, his wheat and corn harvests had pulled in $10,000 less than the crops had cost to grow.

"If we don't get some help then there aren't going to be any family farms," Ochsner said. "And if we go, then this country might as well close the doors."

A few pent-up farmers spun wheels, torched an old tractor, rumbled into the reflecting pool, and drove up the steps of the Ulysses S. Grant Memorial.

"We're all impounded in here," someone yelled.

American Agriculture Movement protesters burn an old tractor near the US Capitol.

THE TRACTORS ARE HERE !
A. A. M.
is FOR REAL ! ! !

MISSOURI

8630

JOHN DEERE

American Agriculture Movement protesters wanted to be taken seriously.

Police in riot gear wielding clubs and gas masks poured out of school buses. A Georgia farmer went blind when a tear gas canister exploded in his tractor cab.

"I didn't come up here to get killed," Hershell Essary of New Mexico said after police sprayed him with pepper spray. "I came to talk to politicians."

Farm leaders from each state huddled and tended a plan.

"We have to impress Washington with our sincerity," said Lyle Davidson, a movement spokesman.

Farmers flocked to Washington, DC, from at least forty states.

Dustin Covey, a Kansas four-year-old, naps during a Senate Agriculture Committee hearing.

Farmers crowded congressional hearings. But would lawmakers listen?

"You would write up your testimonies and they'd just take your paper and throw it down," said Ed Scheufler of Kansas. Bob Bergland, the US Secretary of Agriculture, accused the farmers of "old-fashioned greed" on national television. He feared that higher crop prices would make groceries more expensive.

Secretary of Agriculture Bob Bergland (left) and President Jimmy Carter (right) in the Oval Office of the White House.

Some farmers booed at Bergland. *Not true!* Each loaf of bread used only a few pennies' worth of wheat!

The farmers needed their own interview. David Senter knew how to snag one: by revving the biggest, rumbliest tractor of all.

Dustin Covey, on his pedal tractor, led another protest that featured a toy—a tractorcade to the White House.

Word spread that the farmers were going to bust into the Department of Agriculture.

A twelve-ton tractor inched menacingly toward the building. Police braced for a fight.

"Here comes the tractor," someone yelled.

As cameras rolled, someone busted in, all right. A little boy with a toy tractor slipped past the riot gear, right through the door.

"We didn't say what size tractor we were going to drive," Senter said.

Inching toward the US Department of Agriculture building

On the Mall, the farmers' propane supplies were running low. Their campers' toilet tanks were freezing. Antsy for change, they fired up 250 tractors and paraded to the Lincoln Memorial on the anniversary of President Abraham Lincoln's birth on a Kentucky farm.

"This memorial was built in the name of a farmer," said "Wagonmaster" Gerald McCathern, the Texas farmer who steered the first tractor into DC. "We're going to stay here (in Washington) until the snow stops and the songbirds go to singing."

The farmers pocketed their keys and demanded a meeting with President Jimmy Carter—the most powerful farmer of all.

Lincoln Memorial, February 12, 1979

A woman and child participate in a tractorcade in Washington, DC.

Farm debt drove AAM protesters to DC and followed them home.

But President Carter never showed. A week of protesting had brought no progress for the farmers, and they were running out of ideas.

"It's just as silly for a tractor to be in the streets of Washington as a skyscraper in my cornfield," said Leonard Cox of Kansas. "But we wouldn't have drawn attention to the plight of the family farmer any other way."

The spring thaw loomed. Some farmers began to load up and leave Washington, but winter only tightened its grip.

Snow piled knee-high while the city slept in for the Presidents' Day holiday. The worst blizzard in fifty-seven years was shutting down DC—even more than the tractors had.

Ambulances slid. Tow trucks got stuck. Snowplows slammed into one another.

Heavy snowfall hampers traffic, except for the occasional cross-country skier.

How would the people get help? How could doctors
and nurses reach the sick and injured?

The farmers produced a plan . . .

Police ride snowmobiles after the Presidents' Day
snowstorm, February 18–19, 1979.

. . . to send in the tractors.

They winched ambulances and cars out of snowbanks. Hauled doctors and nurses to work. Helped a heart attack victim. Delivered medicine.

For two days, the tractors toiled. They ferried firetrucks. Burrowed out buses. Chauffeured congress members to work, and grandmas to grocery stores.

Farmers cleared parking lots at hospitals, newspaper buildings, and government offices—even Bob Bergland's Department of Agriculture.

"They have shown themselves to be the best kind of neighbors in a storm," a *Washington Post* editorial read.

Somehow, the snow had cooled tempers.

Towing a stranded car

As the snow melted, the tractors paraded around the White House while playing a different tune: "God Bless America."

"We're with you all the way," a boy yelled.

Locals carried groceries and cookies into the farmers' encampment. Some offered to do the farmers' laundry. People were starting to understand how much they needed farmers. Their message had begun to set roots—but their work in Washington wasn't finished.

Celebrating during a tractorcade permitted by police

A month of tractor traffic had mangled the Mall.

"There's no turf left," said George Berklacy of the National Park Service. "It's nonexistent."

So the farmers cultivated a plan . . .

Aerial view of the Capitol facing tractors on the National Mall

Gerald McCathern of Texas turns the Mall soil to prepare it for grass seed.

. . . to send in the tractors. One last time.

They made their first spring planting: grass seeds on the Mall lawn.

Birds chirped. Green grew. They had done what they could.

"I think my tractor wants to go home," said Leonard Cox of Kansas.

"It wants to go back where it can breathe free."

The farmers knew the fight for fair crop prices would continue.

43

Many farms closed in the 1980s because they couldn't pay their bills.

Several months after the tractor parades, David Senter left his Texas cotton fields for a job that paid—as the American Agriculture Movement's first coordinator in DC. Since then the farmers' plight had worsened. Sunday newspapers listed three or four pages of farm sales each week. Growers lined up for food stamps to feed themselves. Farmers took their own lives out of despair.

Senter thought about how the tractor parades had inspired the people of Washington, DC, to help the farmers corralled on the Mall.

How can we bring back the news cameras? Senter wondered.

Then he knew: by leading farmers back to the Mall.

AAM "March for Parity," Washington, DC, March 1985. Standing right to left: Billy Senter (David Senter's son), Corky Jones, David Senter, and Amy Senter (David's daughter).

Seven hundred desperate farmers planted crosses on the Mall to make it look like a graveyard. The crosses represented the estimated 360 farms disappearing each day.

Images of the protest shook someone who could get people to listen. While on the road, country singer Willie Nelson had passed farm equipment lined up for auction. He called David with an idea:

Let's have a show!

The American Agriculture Movement's "March for Parity"

Farm Aid founders Neil Young, Willie Nelson, and John Cougar Mellencamp

More than fifty famous country and rock acts descended on Illinois corn country for Willie's concert. "Farm Aid" blasted the farmers' message to the nation.

"All of a sudden, here's Willie Nelson and here's eighty thousand people on their feet," Senter said. "All of a sudden, we realized we're not in this alone."

Sixty thousand callers an hour wanted to eat. They pledged donations to the tune of $7 million.

Farm Aid's mission had struck a chord with millions of people—including members of Congress.

The farmers cheered a plan . . .

Farm Aid, Champaign, Illinois, September 22, 1985

. . . to unify.

Meeting notices adorned bulletin boards in feed stores, churches, and supermarkets.

"It's going to take a united effort to stop the going-out-of-business sale currently under way in rural America," wrote Toni Kelley, one of the organizers.

Nearly twenty thousand farmers flocked to six hundred gatherings around the country, made possible by donations

Wayne Baker (left) and David Senter,
Omaha, Nebraska, fall 1986

52

to Farm Aid. Delegates elected at those meetings headed to the big one: the United Farmer and Rancher Congress.

There in St. Louis, farmers voted on their priorities as one. Then they passed recommendations for fair-price policies up the chain to the US Congress—the only national body with the power to write laws.

Ralph Reid (left) and Jerry Grapp, Waterloo, Iowa, summer 1986

A decade after tractors first paraded, lawmakers listened.

The US Congress approved the Agricultural Credit Act of 1987, a loan rescue package that let farmers stay on their farms, even when they couldn't afford to repay the bank.

The farmers who had planted a movement finally reaped its harvest: the end of the crisis. They celebrated by climbing behind the wheel, easing into the fields, and sowing their hope for the future.

Today each US farm feeds about 165 people per year, according to the American Farm Bureau.

David L. Senter and grandson Colten Senter in downtown Chicago to celebrate Farm Aid's twentieth anniversary in 2005

AUTHOR'S NOTE

At the height of the American Agriculture Movement (AAM) in the late 1970s and early 1980s, an estimated two million farmers participated in or supported the cause. One of the loudest and most sustained voices has been David L. Senter's.

After the 1979 protests on the Mall, "the writing was on the wall for my farm," he said in a phone interview. David had grown wheat, cotton, oats, and sorghum; operated a dairy; and raised one hundred other cattle for beef outside Burleson, Texas, south of Fort Worth.

David became one of the original organizers of the American Agriculture Movement in Texas, and later, the nation. After leading Texans to DC and speaking around the country, David dived into a new but related line of work as AAM's first paid national coordinator.

"If Congress had listened—if they would have dealt with the situation—we would not have had that crisis in the '80s," David said. "Go to these rural areas and take a look at these small little towns. There might be a Dollar General and a little quick shop and everything else is boarded up . . . churches are closed. Schools are consolidated. It's like skeletons left on the landscape."

Congress may not have listened at first, but Farm Aid did. The charity amplified producers' voices in 1986 by sponsoring the United Farmer and Rancher Congress, a gathering in St. Louis of 1,900 delegates from around the country to set agriculture policy priorities.

"Farmers came together and put forward 'here's what we think Congress should do,'" David said. Then lawmakers in the US Congress drafted legislation based on the delegates' suggestions. Ultimately, this gave rise to the Agricultural Credit Act of 1987, approved and signed into law by President Ronald Reagan in 1988.

"It stopped the hemorrhaging out there, and the restructuring for the producers to work through their debt," David said. "That was a major turning point."

Those measures helped keep farmers in business and ended the crisis by 1990. Today, David remains active in lobbying farm policy. He was elected the American Agriculture Movement president in 2017.

"I still want to know where my food comes from and want to know there's families producing it," he said. "This is a way I can try to help the next generation."

David also continues to volunteer with Farm Aid, a charity that has raised more than $50 million for agricultural producers over thirty-five years of nearly annual concerts. "We're going to do it until the problem's solved," David said.

At the time of this writing in 2019, farmers were seeing low crop prices again, in part because of a trade war between the US and China. In an attempt to force China to change unfair trade policies, President Donald Trump directed the US to impose steep tariffs, or taxes, on a range of Chinese goods coming into the US. In return, China placed tariffs on US goods, including agricultural products, making them more expensive for consumers there. China had been the largest buyer of American soybeans when it temporarily quit buying them. Because demand for US soybeans fell, the selling price for farmers tumbled.

Congress has never approved a law that guarantees farmers parity, or a selling price above the cost of production. That differs from most industries, where the producer sets the price for a product.

"Parity would have allowed us to keep up with what fuel was costing and interest rates and would have allowed farmers the purchasing power," David said. "It would have prevented the complete crash in the '80s. We're going to lose as big a percentage of farmers this time.

"It's a race to the bottom on prices . . . you're losing money on every bushel. But you know, low prices are worldwide and it's strangling farmers everywhere."

In 1935, the nation had almost seven million farms, according to US Census records. Now there are about two million.

Expenses continue to rise. Crop prices haven't kept up with inflation, but with modern technologies, family farms have managed by growing in size and producing higher crop yields than ever before.

US FARM PRICES THROUGH THE YEARS

Income

Average price for a bushel of wheat:	A bushel of corn:	A bushel of soybeans:
1974: $4.09	1974: $3.02	1974: $6.64
1977: $2.33	1977: $2.05	1977: $5.88
2012: $7.77 (all-time high)	2012: $6.89 (all-time high)	2012: $14.40 (all-time high)
2019: $4.70	2019: $3.85	2019: $9.00

—US Department of Agriculture historical averages. Prices vary depending on location.

Expenses

New combine harvester:
1974: $21,000
1977: $41,200
2019: $400,000–600,000

—1970s prices from McCathern, Gentle Rebels; 2019 prices from Fastline.com and PrairieLand Partners, Concordia, Kansas.

Average yield in bushels per acre

Wheat:	Corn:	Soybeans:
1977: 30.7	1977: 90.9	1977: 30.6
2018: 47.6	2018: 176.4	2018: 51.6

—US Department of Agriculture

FARM PROTEST TIMELINE

January 1977: Jimmy Carter, a Georgia peanut farmer, becomes president.

1977: Average wheat farmer in the United States pays $3.55 to grow a single bushel of wheat that sells for $2.50 or less.

September 1977: A handful of farmers in Campo, Colorado, organize a strike to increase demand for grain and drive prices higher.

Thanksgiving 1977: Eleven thousand seven hundred tractors and twenty thousand farmers protest in Plains, Georgia, Carter's hometown. Carter spends the weekend at Camp David in Maryland.

December 1977: David Senter joins one thousand tractors in protest at the Texas state capitol building in Austin. On this day, one hundred thousand tractors descend on farm-state capitals around the country.

January 1978: Congress convenes for a new session while fifty thousand farmers protest low crop prices in Washington, DC.

April 1978: Senate-approved measure to raise wheat, feed grain, cotton, and soybean prices fails in the House of Representatives.

May 1978: President Carter signs the Emergency Agricultural Act into law, but many farmers believe it doesn't go far enough to help them.

January 13–16, 1979: Tractors from all over the country set off toward Washington, DC, covering an average of one hundred miles a day. The routes reach up to thirty miles in length and sometimes require a hundred football fields' worth of space for parking each evening.

February 5, 1979: Ten thousand tractors, farm trucks, and campers roll into Washington, DC.

February 19, 1979: Presidents' Day blizzard dumps twenty inches of snow on Washington, DC. Tractors help dig out the city.

January 1981: Ronald Reagan becomes president.

September 1985: Singers Willie Nelson, John Cougar Mellencamp, and Neil Young host more than fifty musical acts for the first Farm Aid concert in Champaign, Illinois. Eighty thousand people attend, and millions watch on television. Over $7 million is raised for farmers. The money funds a crisis hotline, counseling, lawyers' fees for farmers fighting for their land in court, and the upcoming United Farmer and Rancher Congress.

December 1985: Reagan signs the Food Security Act of 1985, a five-year bill from Congress that would pay farmers when market prices fell too low to cover production costs.

September 1986: Farm Aid hosts the United Farmer and Rancher Congress, a gathering in St. Louis of one thousand nine hundred delegates from around the country to set agriculture policy priorities.

January 1988: Reagan signs the Agricultural Credit Act of 1987, the US Congress's loan rescue package that would help prevent farm foreclosures.

January 1989: George Herbert Walker Bush becomes president.

1990: Various farm advocacy groups declare the farm crisis to be over following implementation of the loan rescue package.

American Agriculture Movement protest buttons

SOURCE NOTES

The source of each quotation in this book is found below. The citation indicates the first words of the quotation and its document source. The sources are listed in the bibliography.

"When a bushel . . .": Fred Bartels, quoted in Potter

"You bet we started . . .": Marjory Scheufler, "Optimist Club"

"Apathy is going . . .": Marjory Scheufler, "Kiwanis"

"faster [than] crab grass": Marjory Scheufler, "Optimist Club"

"We've got to have . . .": Tommy Kersey, quoted in *Indianapolis Star*

"This is the worst . . .": unidentified "radio newsman," quoted in Yoho, "Tractorcade"

"We only want . . .": George Burrows, quoted in *Greenville (AL) Advocate*

"They lost my vote": Ben White, quoted in Feaver

"guarantees us something . . .": Marcus Everidge, quoted in Davis and Washington

"Get 'em rollin' . . .": Joe Flanagan, quoted in Feaver

"Our boys just . . .": Wade B. Fleetwood

"We come here . . .": Larry Schmitz, quoted in Dickey and Harden

"If we don't . . .": Ken Ochsner, quoted in Stott

"We're all impounded . . .": unidentified farmer, quoted in Spencer

"I didn't come . . .": Hershell Essary, quoted in Dickey and Harden

"We have to impress . . .": Lyle Davidson, quoted in Marjory Scheufler, "Observations"

"You would write . . .": Edward E. Scheufler

"old-fashioned greed": United Press International, "Farmers Cause Damage"

"Here comes the tractor": unidentified farmer, quoted in Bonner

"We didn't say . . .": Senter, phone interview with the author

"This memorial was built . . .": Gerald McCathern, quoted in Gup

"It's just as silly . . .": Leonard Cox, quoted in Christensen, "Farmers Subdued"

"They have shown . . .": *Washington Post*

"We're with you . . .": Kerney

"There's no turf left . . .": George Berklacy, quoted in Harden and Kerney

"I think my tractor . . .": Leonard Cox, quoted in Christensen, "Farmers Subdued"

"All of a sudden . . .": Senter, from Wilkinson

"It's going to take . . .": Kelley

"the writing was . . .": Senter, phone interview with the author

"If Congress had listened . . .": same as above

"Farmers came together . . .": same as above

"It stopped the . . .": same as above

"I still want . . .": same as above

"We're going to . . .": same as above

"Parity would have . . .": same as above

"It's a race . . .": same as above

PRIMARY SOURCES/INTERVIEWS

Anderson, Beverly Snyder. "1979 Tractorcade to Washington, D.C.: Interview with Beverly Snyder Anderson." By Joan Weaver and Rosetta Graff, Kinsley Library, November 3, 2012. kinsleylibrary.info/tractorcade-to-dc/tractorcade-interviewees/.

Derley, Lester. "1979 Tractorcade to Washington, D.C.: Interview with Lester Derley." By Joan Weaver and Rosetta Graff, Kinsley Library, December 3, 2012. kinsleylibrary.info/tractorcade-to-dc/tractorcade-interviewees/.

Fleetwood, Wade B. Letter to the editor. *Washington Post*, February 10, 1979.

McCathern, Gerald. *Gentle Rebels*. Hereford, Texas: Food for Thought Publications, 1982.

Miller, Darrel. "1979 Tractorcade to Washington, D.C.: Interview with Darrel Miller." By Joan Weaver and Rosetta Graff, Kinsley Library, August 28, 2012. kinsleylibrary.info/tractorcade-to-dc/tractorcade-interviewees/.

Scheufler, Edward, and Marjory Scheufler. "Report on Tractorcade to Washington D.C." kinsleylibrary.info/tractorcade-to-dc/tractorcade-interviewees/.

Scheufler, Edward E. "1979 Tractorcade to Washington D.C.: Interview with Edward E. Scheufler." By Joan Weaver and Rosetta Graff, Kinsley Library, September 24, 2012. kinsleylibrary.info/tractorcade-to-dc/tractorcade-interviewees/.

Scheufler, Marjory. "Kiwanis Mar. 19th." American Agriculture Movement, Tractorcade speaker from Kansas, March 19, 1979. kinsleylibrary.info/tractorcade-to-dc/tractorcade-interviewees/.

———. "Observations from Washington D.C. Jan. 21 thru Jan. 25 [1978]." American Agriculture Movement, Tractorcade speaker from Kansas. kinsleylibrary.info/tractorcade-to-dc/tractorcade-interviewees/.

———. "Optimist Club: July 19, 1978." American Agriculture Movement, Tractorcade speaker from Kansas, July 19, 1978. kinsleylibrary.info/tractorcade-to-dc/tractorcade-interviewees/.

———. "St. Bernards Mar. 18." American Agriculture Movement, Tractorcade speaker from Kansas, March 18, 1979. kinsleylibrary.info/tractorcade-to-dc/tractorcade-interviewees/.

Schinstock, Mary Ellen. "1979 Tractorcade to Washington, D.C.: Interview with Mary Ellen Schinstock." By Joan Weaver and Rosetta Graff, October 10, 2012. kinsleylibrary.info/tractorcade-to-dc/tractorcade-interviewees/.

Senter, David. Oral History Interview, January 5, 2014. Interview by Andy Wilkinson, Online Transcription, Texas Tech University Southwest Collection/Special Collections Library.

———. Phone interview with the author, July 24, 2017.

Snyder, Beverly. "Tractorcade to Washington, DC Diary: January 18–February 8, 1979." kinsleylibrary.info/tractorcade-to-dc/tractorcade-interviewees/.

Titus, Jean. "1979 Tractorcade to Washington D.C.: Interview with Jean Titus." By Joan Weaver and Rosetta Graff, Kinsley Library, October 3, 2012. kinsleylibrary.info/tractorcade-to-dc/tractorcade-interviewees/.

PRIMARY SOURCES/NEWS

"American Agriculture Movement Historical Calendar." Iredell, TX: American Agriculture Movement, 1983.

Associated Press. "AAM Tractorcade May Be Farmers' Last Hope." *Burlington (NC) Times-News*, January 30, 1979.

Bercovici, Liza. "Final Tractorcade Brings Harmony." *Washington Post*, March 2, 1979.

Bonner, Miller. "Farmers' Week in Washington . . ." *Paris (TX) News*, February 11, 1979.

Brasch, Sam. "When Tractors Invaded D.C." *Modern Farmer*, February 5, 2014. modernfarmer.com/2014/02/living-legacy-d-c-tractorcade-35-years-later/.

Brazil (IN) Times. "Tractorcade Rolling Along." January 27, 1979.

Christensen, Jean. "Farmers Subdued, Behaved for Last Tractorcade." *Hutchinson (KS) News*, March 2, 1979.

———. "Scott City Couple Arrested During DC Tractorcade." *Garden City (KS) Telegram*, February 26, 1979.

Coleman, Milton, and J. Regan Kerney. "Farmers Are Told to Have Tractors Off Mall Tonight." *Washington Post*, February 28, 1979.

Crampton, Betty. "Snow, Cold Stall Tractorcade." *Salina (KS) Journal*, January 24, 1979.

Cumberland (MD) Evening Times. "Farm Group Plans Frederick 'reunion.'" February 2, 1979.

Davis, Michael D., and Adrienne Washington. "Farmers Clash with Police at the Capitol." *Washington Star*, February 5, 1979.

Dickey, Christopher, and Blaine Harden. "Pent-Up, Angry Farmers Taunt Police." *Washington Post*, February 7, 1979.

Feaver, Douglas B. "Protesting Farmers Snarl City's Traffic." *Washington Post*, February 6, 1979.

Fisher, Don. "Violence Reported as Tractorcade Moves into Capitol." *Paris (TX) News*, February 5, 1979.

Fuson, Ken, and Larry Fruhling. "Music, Money, Mist Shower over Farmers at Farm Aid Concert." *Des Moines Register*, September 23, 1985.

Greene, Donald Miller. "The American Agriculture Movement: Its Cause, Spread, and Impact." Norman: University of Oklahoma Graduate College, 1979.

Greenville (AL) Advocate. "AAM'ers to Become Lobbyists." January 25, 1979.

Gup, Ted. "Farmers Move 250 Tractors to Lincoln Memorial." *Washington Post*, February 13, 1979. washingtonpost.com/ archive/local/1979/02/13/farmers-move-250-tractors-to-lincoln-memorial/6e5e7340-c82f-41ef-a36e-4e47b233c93d/?utm_term=. a6be66ca7864.

Gup, Ted, and Dan Morgan. "Tractor Caravan Disrupts Some Traffic." *Washington Post*, February 7, 1979.

Harden, Blaine. "Protesting Farmers Snarl City's Traffic." *Washington Post*, February 6, 1979.

Harden, Blaine, and Regan Kerney. "Mall Damage Estimated at $2 Million." *Washington Post*, February 10, 1979.

Hutchinson (KS) News. "Tractorcade Schedule Moved Ahead a Week." January 3, 1979.

Indianapolis Star. "Hey Good Buddy, Farmers in Convoy Are Serious for Sure." January 29, 1979.

Junker, Wes, and Jeff Halverson. "How the Surprise President's Day Snowstorm of 1979 Advanced Forecasting." *Washington Post*, February 16, 2015. washingtonpost.com/news/capital-weather-gang/ wp/2015/02/16/how-the-surprise-presidents-day-snowstorm-of-1979-advanced-the-science-of-forecasting/?noredirect=on&utm_term=. b6a43ca0442b.

Kerney, J. Regan. "Farmers' Snow Deeds Earn Them New Friends." *Washington Post*, February 22, 1979. washingtonpost.com/ archive/local/1979/02/22/farmers-snow-deeds-earn-them-new-friends/631f9031-9029-4644-9dd9-8cd4aefded7a/?utm_term=. dbf886412d61.

King, Brian B. "Farmers Converge on Washington." *Paris (TX) News*, February 5, 1979.

Macy, Robert. "Tractorcade Makes K.C. for Evening Rush Hour." *Iola (KS) Register*, January 20, 1979.

New York Times. "Farm Population Lowest Since 1850's." July 20, 1988. nytimes.com/1988/07/20/us/farm-population-lowest-since-1850-s.html.

News (Frederick, MD). "There's a Lot of Snow When Even the Tow Truck Is Stuck." February 20, 1979.

Potter, Dan. "Tractorcade Stops over in Sedalia." *Sedalia (MO) Democrat*, January 21, 1979.

Pulitzer, Joseph IV. "Farmer Claims Vindication in Protest." *St. Louis Post-Dispatch*, February 8, 1981.

Ringle, Ken. "Farmers Asked to Help Pay $950,000 in Mall Damage." *Washington Post*, March 10, 1979.

Risen, James. "After Crisis, Farm Economy Growing Again." *Los Angeles Times*, August 12, 1990.

Seminole (TX) Sentinel. "County Farmers Continue National March." January 28, 1979.

Spencer, Duncan. "Leaders, Police Reach Agreement on Tractorcade to White House." *Washington Star*, February 6, 1979.

——. "Protest Cost Nears $1 Million." *Washington Star*, February 9, 1979.

Stott, Charlie. "'A Rough Old Road' in More Ways Than One." *Morning Herald (Hagerstown, MD)*, February 3, 1979.

Sweezy, Martha. *A Report on the United Farmer & Rancher Congress: September 11–13, 1986, St. Louis, MO, 1–21*. Cambridge, MA: Farm Aid, 1986. 1efnyhsj63r2fo5g01erbmcv-wpengine.netdna-ssl.com/wp-content/uploads/2015/08/United-Farmer-Rancher-Congress.pdf.

United Press International. "Farm Aid Music Raises Millions." *Hawk Eye* (Burlington, Iowa), September 23, 1985.

United States Department of Agriculture, National Agricultural Statistics Service. "Farmers Cause Damage to Farm Organization Office." *Athens (AL) News Courier*, February 9, 1979.

——. "Storm Gives Farmers a Chance to Be Heroes." *Salina (KS) Journal*, February 20, 1979.

——. "Storm Paralyzes East Coast Areas." *Cumberland (MD) Evening Times*, February 20, 1979.

Washington Post. "The Farmers and the Snow." February 21, 1979.

Yoho, Bob. "AAM Farmers Hear Tough Talk." *Hutchinson (KS) News*, November 30, 1978.

——. "'Cade' Must Have Radios to Pass the Word." *Hutchinson (KS) News*, January 29, 1979.

——. "Farmers Prime Tractors and AAM Spirit." *Hutchinson (KS) News*, November 19, 1978.

——. "Kansan Says Tractorcade 'Like a Dream.'" *Hutchinson (KS) News*, February 17, 1979.

——. "Tractorcade Snarls Kansas City Traffic." *Hutchinson (KS) News*, January 20, 1979.

——. "Tractors Surround Washington." *Hutchinson (KS) News*, February 3, 1979.

OTHER SOURCES

Associated Press. "Former Secretary Bob Bergland Dies at 90." Drovers.com, December 9, 2018. drovers.com/article/former-agriculture-secretary-bob-bergland-dies-90.

Crapanzano, Christina. "A Brief History of Farm Aid." *Time*, October 1, 2010. content.time.com/time/arts/article/0,8599,2023006,00.html.

Farm Aid. "Farm Aid: A Concert for America—Complete TV Broadcast." Performed by Willie Nelson, Neil Young, John Cougar Mellencamp, and others. YouTube video. First aired on television September 22, 1985. youtube.com/watch?v=hO7gdTWqEiw.

Kelley, Toni. "Welcome to the United Farmer and Rancher Congress." In *The United Farmer & Rancher Congress: 1986, "Strengthening the Spirit of America,"* edited by George Naylor, 1. Cambridge, MA: Farm Aid, 1986. 1efnyhsj63r2fo5g01erbmcv-wpengine.netdna-ssl.com/wp-content/uploads/2015/08/UFRC-program.pdf.

Llewelyn, Rich. Kansas State University Department of Agricultural Economics. "Corn Supply and Demand Spreadsheet (WASDE)." World Agricultural Supply and Demand Estimates, United States Department of Agriculture. Accessed December 10, 2019. agmanager.info/grain-marketing/grain-supply-and-demand-wasde/us-supply-and-demand-wasde-spreadsheets.

——. "Soybean Supply and Demand Spreadsheet (WASDE)." World Agricultural Supply and Demand Estimates, United States Department of Agriculture. Accessed December 10, 2019. agmanager.info/grain-marketing/grain-supply-and-demand-wasde/us-supply-and-demand-wasde-spreadsheets.

——. "Wheat Supply and Demand Spreadsheet (WASDE)." World Agricultural Supply and Demand Estimates, United States Department of Agriculture. Accessed December 10, 2019. agmanager.info/grain-marketing/grain-supply-and-demand-wasde/us-supply-and-demand-wasde-spreadsheets.

National Association of Wheat Growers. "Wheat Facts." Accessed September 19, 2019. wheatworld.org/wheat-101/wheat-facts/.

Patoski, Joe Nick. *Willie Nelson: An Epic Life*. New York: Back Bay, 2008.

United States Department of Agriculture, National Agricultural Statistics Service. "U.S. Farm Production Expenditures, 2017." NASS *Highlights*, August 2018. nass.usda.gov/Publications/Highlights/2018/2017_Farm_Production_Expenditures.pdf.

ACKNOWLEDGMENTS

Special thanks goes to David L. Senter, who shared details of his life through interviews and reviewed this manuscript; to Dean Holbert and Donna Covey, who lent their scrapbooks, memorabilia, and memories; to Larry Matlack, Gerald McCathern, and Darrel Miller, who were instrumental with the tractorcades; to Lacee Hoelting, director of the Bayer Museum of Agriculture, which features an American Agriculture Movement Heritage exhibit in Lubbock, Texas; and to the Kinsley (Kansas) Library, which conducted an extensive oral history project about the tractorcades and posted interviews with local participants online at kinsleylibrary.info/tractorcade-to-dc/.

Finally, thanks to my dad, Noel Hanson, for feeding the nation as a lifetime farmer, for critiquing this story, and for shaking loose his memory of attending a 1970s farm strike. And thanks to my brothers, Troy and Scott Hanson, and my mom, Gloria Hanson, for dedicating themselves to feeding us all for the foreseeable future.

PICTURE CREDITS

AP Images: 1, 9, 19, 34.
AP/Bob Daugherty: 42.
AP/Harvey Georges: 12.
AP/Jeff Taylor: 18, 41, 43.
AP/John Duricka: 26.
AP/Scott Stewart: 49.
AP/Thumma: 10.
Bayer Museum of Agriculture: 58, 63, 64.
Bettmann/Getty Images: 50.
Darrel Miller: 29.
© David Peterson: 44, 52, 53, 54.
DC Public Library, Star Collection © Washington Post: 17, 37, 39.
Farm Aid, Inc.: 51, 56.
Jimmy Carter Presidential Library, White House Staff Photographer Collection, C-12865, September 10, 1979: 27.
© Jo Freeman, 1979, jofreeman.com: 28, 33.
© Ken Hawkins, KenHawkinsPictures.com: 3, 7.
Linda Wheeler/*Washington Post* via Getty Images: 20.
Martha Tabor photograph, courtesy of Larry Matlack/American Agriculture Movement: 47.
Smithsonian Institution Archives: SIA Acc. 11-009 [79-1675], Created by Hofmeister, Richard K: 22, 24. SIA Acc. 11-009 [79-1688], Created by Tinsley, Jeff: 25.
Thomas J. O'Halloran, U.S. News & World Report Magazine Photograph Collection, Library of Congress, LC-U9-35542-15: 4.
United States Department of Agriculture: 14, 32.
United States Park Police photograph, courtesy of Darrel Miller: 31.
© Wally McNamee/Corbis via Getty Images: Cover

Calkins Creek
An imprint of Boyds Mills & Kane, a division of Astra Publishing House
calkinscreekbooks.com

Printed in China
ISBN: 978-1-68437-908-8
Library of Congress Control Number: 2019953788
First edition

10 9 8 7 6 5 4 3 2 1

Design by Barbara Grzeslo
The text is set in Futura.